How to Start a Food Truck Business

Step by Step Guide to Start a Profitable Food Truck Business, from Wonderful Marketing Strategy, to Plans, Startup and all You Need to Succeed

David Werner

Copyright

Copyright ©2024 David Werner. All rights reserved

Table of content

COPYRIGHT

ABSTRACT

INTRODUCTION

Chapter 1: The Food Truck Business

Chapter 2: Key Elements of Food Truck Success

Chapter 3: Crafting a Marketing Strategy for Your Food Truck

Chapter 4: Crafting a Comprehensive Food Truck Proposal

Chapter 5: Attracting Customers to Your Food Truck

Chapter 6: Building Connections and Publicity

Chapter 7: Naming Your Food Truck

Chapter 8: Crafting Your Food Truck Menu

- **Best Practices** for Food Truck Menu Design
- Creating Your Food Truck **Menu**

Chapter 9: Establishing Your Food Truck Brand

Understanding Branding

- Developing Your Food Truck Brand Identity
- Maintaining Consistency Across Channels

Chapter 10: Determining the Ideal Number of Menu Items for Your Food Truck

Chapter 11: Top-Selling Food Truck Items

Chapter 12: Selecting Profitable Food for Your Food Truck

Chapter 13: Assessing Food Truck Profitability

Chapter 14: Identifying Risk Factors

Chapter 15: Understanding the Primary Objective of a Food Truck

Conclusion

Abstract

Discover the essential steps to launch a successful food truck business with this comprehensive guide. From crafting an effective marketing strategy to detailed plans for startup and operations, this resource equips aspiring entrepreneurs with everything necessary to thrive in the competitive world of mobile cuisine.

INTRODUCTION

Crafting Effective Marketing Strategies for Your Food Truck Business

For individuals possessing culinary prowess or a fervent love for gastronomy, the aspiration of launching and managing their own restaurant often looms large. However, the traditional route of establishing a brick-and-mortar eatery demands substantial initial investments that surpass the means of many.

Fortunately, an alternative avenue exists for aspiring chefs—the burgeoning food truck market. Food trucks present a more accessible entry point into the culinary realm, significantly reducing the financial barriers associated with launching a conventional restaurant.

Moreover, the success of food trucks frequently paves the way for brand expansion, with possibilities ranging from extending services to additional food delivery locations to ultimately establishing a standalone restaurant.

For those intrigued by the prospect, comprehensive guidance awaits to navigate the journey of initiating a thriving food truck enterprise.

In this Comprehensive Guide, you'll discover:

- What makes a food truck successful?
- Is a food truck a good business?
- How do I write a marketing plan for a food truck?
- What's a good name for a food truck?
- What type of food trucks make the most money?
- What is the most successful food for food trucks?
- What is the main goal of a food truck?
- Who is the target market for food trucks?
- How many items should you have on a food truck menu?
- How do you write a food truck menu?
- What sells best on food trucks?
- What food items are high profit?
- Where is the best place to start a food truck?
- And much More!

Embarking on the journey of devising impactful marketing strategies for your food truck demands careful consideration and strategic planning. This guide will illuminate various avenues you can explore to enhance the visibility and appeal of your mobile culinary venture.

Upon perusing this manual, you'll gain insights into diverse marketing tactics tailored specifically for food trucks. Armed with this knowledge, you'll be equipped to commence the development of your tailored marketing approach, positioning your business for success.

It's worth noting that while marketing for a new business may seem daunting, particularly in the culinary domain, the arduous groundwork of establishing your food truck—procuring permits, securing equipment, and navigating regulatory processes—is already accomplished. Hence, the marketing phase should be approached with confidence, viewing it as a manageable aspect of your entrepreneurial journey.

Chapter 1

The Food Truck Business

Launching a food truck business requires meticulous attention to product safety and adherence to sanitary standards, especially given the unique challenges of mobile food service. Selecting the right vehicle is paramount; while true food trucks are rare and costly, many entrepreneurs opt to convert old vans into mobile kitchens.

Food trucks come in two primary forms: buses and trailers. For simplicity and ease of transportation, purchasing a pre-converted trailer is often preferable. Once acquired, securing a trade permit from the local mayor's office is essential, followed by obtaining necessary permits from regulatory bodies.

Crafting a distinct brand identity, conceptualizing the menu, and considering seasonal variations are crucial steps in establishing a successful food truck. Tailoring offerings to suit seasonal demand ensures relevance and customer satisfaction year-round.

Chapter 2

Key Elements of Food Truck Success

A food truck, essentially a mobile snack bar, offers numerous advantages, including mobility and a popular product selection. Six expert tips can enhance entrepreneurs' efforts in running a thriving business centered on serving delicious and affordable food.

Operating a mobile food establishment proves lucrative in today's fast-paced lifestyle, where homemade meals are often impractical. Whether it's a quick breakfast on the way to work or a weekend indulgence, food trucks cater to the needs of busy consumers seeking convenience.

While summer sees a surge in demand for mobile eateries, the challenge lies in sustaining business during colder months when foot traffic dwindles. Adaptation becomes paramount to retain and attract clientele, prompting entrepreneurs to explore innovative strategies to weather seasonal fluctuations.

Outlined below are six actionable tips aimed at empowering food truck owners to not only endure but thrive year-round:

1. Assess Your Situation: Identify your strengths and unique selling points to devise a winter survival strategy tailored to your business.

2. Learn from Peers: Engage with fellow mobile food vendors to gain insights and inspiration for winter business plans.

3. Customer Engagement: Solicit feedback and suggestions from patrons to tailor offerings and enhance the cold-weather dining experience.

By leveraging strengths, learning from industry peers, and actively engaging with customers, food truck operators can fortify their businesses against seasonal challenges and foster year-round success.

Preparing for the Winter Season: Six Essential Tips

1. Prioritize Staff Comfort: In addition to catering to customers, ensure the well-being of your team, whose demeanor reflects your business. Invest in specialized winter attire with branded logos to keep them warm and cheerful during chilly shifts. Seek input from employees to optimize food truck insulation for prolonged exposure.

2. Explore Catering Opportunities: Extend your reach by offering catering services for various

events, from youth gatherings to birthdays, allowing consistent sales of your signature dishes year-round. While similarities exist between food truck and catering operations, be prepared to develop additional skills to excel in this expanded service.

3. Target Mass Events: Seize the opportunity to cater to large crowds at sports competitions, cultural festivals, and seasonal celebrations, where attendees eagerly seek snacks and refreshments for themselves and their children.

4. Forge Partnerships: Collaborate with complementary businesses, such as bars or restaurants lacking food options, to mutually benefit from cross-promotion. Specialize your offerings to fill gaps in their menus, whether savory snacks or delectable desserts.

5. Embrace Seasonal Fare: Combat winter blues by introducing festive seasonal dishes, creatively packaged to entice guests despite inclement

weather. Showcase culinary creativity with traditional delights like pancakes for Maslenitsa.

6. Secure a Fixed Location: Ensure stability during non-event periods by negotiating long-term agreements with businesses willing to host your food truck, guaranteeing a steady customer flow. Offer incentives like complimentary beverages or employee discounts to entice cooperation.

In the dynamic world of mobile fast food, adaptability is key to enduring success. Embrace new opportunities, maintain strategic partnerships, and innovate your menu to outshine competitors and thrive regardless of economic challenges.

Chapter 3

Crafting a Marketing Strategy for Your Food Truck

Launching a food truck business requires meticulous planning and strategic thinking, starting with a comprehensive marketing plan. If you've diligently followed the steps to establish your food truck venture, you likely already have the foundation for your strategy in place—a well-thought-out business plan that includes thorough market analysis.

Market Research for Food Trucks:
Conducting market research for a food truck mirrors the process for any other business endeavor. If you've previously owned a business, you're familiar with the basics. However, if you're new to

entrepreneurship, consider exploring resources like guides on restaurant opening for invaluable insights applicable to any food-related enterprise.

Defining Your Target Audience:

Understanding your target demographic is crucial for food truck success. Typically, the primary audience comprises young adults aged 18 to 40, often from middle-class backgrounds, seeking novel culinary experiences and convenience. Crafting detailed buyer personas based on real data enables tailored service delivery, ensuring alignment with customer preferences.

While general trends offer guidance, it's essential to conduct localized research to accurately profile your specific audience. By continually refining your understanding of customer needs and preferences, you can adapt your offerings to maximize appeal and drive business growth.

Crafting Your Branding Strategy

Establishing a strong brand identity is pivotal for promoting a food truck effectively. Once you've pinpointed your target audience and buyer personas, it's imperative to define all aspects of branding, encompassing brand image, colors, logo, tagline, employee attire, and every element influencing the visual and experiential facets of your business.

Brand consistency lends legitimacy and fosters customer recognition and loyalty. Streamlining and defining branding elements facilitate customer familiarity and enhance the overall experience, ultimately contributing to improved customer retention rates.

Identifying Effective Marketing Channels

Location-based marketing holds significant potential for food trucks. Tailoring your marketing channels requires a deep understanding of your customer base:

- Which social media platforms resonate most with your target demographic?
- What types of content and advertising tactics are most engaging?
- How can you leverage paid advertising effectively?
- Should you incorporate email or text message marketing?
- Are Google Maps or location-based marketing viable options?

Strategically Applying Marketing Initiatives

Once you've identified optimal marketing channels, implementation becomes paramount. Create a structured content calendar covering various platforms to maximize your business's visibility and impact. Delegating tasks to a community manager can alleviate the burden and ensure consistency across platforms.

Maintaining a balance between quality and consistency necessitates careful time management and organization. Allocating a marketing budget enables sustained efforts without overwhelming direct responsibilities. Monitoring and analyzing marketing strategies and their outcomes are essential for optimizing results over time and ensuring cost-effectiveness and sustainability.

Innovative Marketing Approaches for Food Trucks

Marketing a food truck requires distinct strategies, diverging from conventional restaurant promotion methods. Establishing a close-knit bond with the local customer base is paramount in this dynamic sector.

Outlined below are effective strategies that yield optimal results while emphasizing consistency over substantial investments, fostering sustainability in food truck marketing endeavors.

1. Harnessing Technological Advancements:

Leverage technology and mobile apps to enhance the convenience factor of your food truck. Given the prevalence of online payment apps among the predominantly youthful clientele, ensure seamless integration of various payment methods.

Moreover, develop a user-friendly website showcasing your menu and current location, facilitating easy access for customers. Utilizing dynamic QR code generators for menu distribution not only reduces printing costs but also aligns with evolving consumer preferences.

Implementing these technological solutions is straightforward and cost-effective:

- Utilize free website generators to establish an online presence.

- Digitize your menu for QR code distribution or website display.
- Enable digital ordering to streamline customer transactions.
- Employ thermal printers for efficient kitchen management.
- Adopt mobile POS systems for hassle-free invoicing and payment processing.
- Offer discounts and accept diverse payment methods to enhance customer convenience.

2. Cultivating Community Engagement:

Foster a sense of community around your food truck to augment its social appeal. Unlike traditional restaurants, food trucks thrive on interpersonal connections akin to bar environments.

Forge relationships within the local community, whether by initiating or joining existing social groups. Engage with diverse segments such as sports teams, corporate entities, residential neighborhoods, and other affinity groups.

Building authentic connections requires genuine engagement and participation in community activities, transcending mere commercial interests:

- Attend community events sans the food truck to demonstrate altruism.
- Volunteer for charitable causes to embed your truck within the community fabric.
- Prioritize transparency and authenticity to resonate with community members.
- Cultivate meaningful relationships to humanize your business and foster loyalty.

By embracing technological innovations and nurturing community ties, food truck operators can cultivate a sustainable marketing approach that resonates with their target audience and fosters long-term success.

3. Leveraging Branding for Merchandising Opportunities

A compelling brand identity provides a lucrative avenue for developing branded merchandise for your food truck. Integrating branded products into your marketing strategy amplifies brand visibility and enhances customer engagement. Diverse merchandise options such as apparel, customized cups, and more resonate with your clientele, fostering brand loyalty and serving as effective marketing tools.

Furthermore, the sale of branded merchandise not only generates additional revenue but also bolsters marketing initiatives. A self-sustaining marketing strategy fueled by merchandise sales enables continuous enhancement of promotional efforts, ensuring long-term business sustainability.

4. Crafting High-Quality Audiovisual Content Across Platforms

In the realm of contemporary marketing, audiovisual content reigns supreme. To captivate and engage a predominantly youthful audience, tailor your content strategy to social media platforms like TikTok, YouTube, Instagram, Twitter, and Facebook (or Meta). Create compelling videos to:

- Showcase your menu offerings, culinary creations, and brand identity.
- Entertain and engage your audience, fostering community interaction.
- Educate customers about your business values, mission, and vision.

Utilizing these platforms strategically enhances brand visibility and fosters deeper connections with your audience, underscoring your business's significance within the community.

5. Implementing Customer Retention Strategies

Customer retention is paramount for sustained success in the food service industry. Deploying effective retention strategies hinges on delivering exceptional customer experiences. Simple yet impactful tactics such as:

- Sending personalized coupons via SMS or email.
- Offering discounts on select menu items.
- Selling convenient and affordable tableware.
- Rolling out regular promotions and incentives.
- Providing additional perks like complimentary drinks upon reaching a certain spending threshold.

These measures cultivate a sense of value and appreciation among customers, fostering loyalty and repeat business. Consistency in service delivery and product quality further solidifies customer trust and ensures long-term patronage.

6. Engage with Live Content and Social Media Presence

Utilize live content to enhance customer engagement and promote your food truck's location. Broadcasting surprise live streams showcasing your current whereabouts and enticing promotions can yield substantial returns, particularly if you've cultivated a loyal community.

Leverage the diverse features of social media platforms like Instagram to diversify your content and maintain regular posting schedules, maximizing your online visibility and audience reach.

Consider expanding your online presence by establishing a YouTube channel or Discord community, contingent upon your target audience's preferences. Utilize these channels to disseminate valuable information, promotions, and updates to your customer base, fostering deeper connections and enhancing brand loyalty.

Adapt your marketing efforts to meet your customers where they are most active and engaged, be it on social media platforms, community forums, or other digital spaces.

Marketing a food truck presents unique challenges compared to traditional brick-and-mortar restaurants. While restaurants enjoy a static location and a predictable customer base, food trucks offer mobility and versatility, allowing them to tap into various communities within their operational radius.

Successfully marketing a food truck requires a dual focus on customer retention and community building. While navigating the dynamic nature of food truck operations presents challenges, it also offers opportunities to connect with diverse communities and foster long-term customer relationships.

Chapter 4

Crafting a Comprehensive Food Truck Proposal

Understanding the Target Audience:
A food truck caters to individuals seeking quick and convenient snack options on the go. The nature of fast food necessitates swift preparation and immediate consumption to maintain flavor and quality. Therefore, the menu should prioritize efficiency in serving dishes, often relying on pre-prepared and semi-prepared ingredients.

To maximize customer reach, the menu should encompass breakfast and lunch options, appealing to nearby employees and families with children. Sweet treats like waffles and child-friendly dishes ensure inclusivity and cater to diverse preferences.

Setting Yourself Apart:

Differentiation is crucial in a competitive market dominated by traditional fast food outlets. Crafting a unique menu that aligns with the truck's overall concept is essential. Moreover, attention-grabbing visual branding enhances customer attraction and retention. A well-designed food truck with a catchy name enhances visibility and draws attention from passersby.

Capitalizing on Events and Festivals:

Participation in local festivals and events presents lucrative opportunities to boost sales and increase visibility. Registering for such events through the administration's website facilitates access to larger crowds and heightened exposure.

Supply Chain Management:

Given space constraints, daily replenishment of supplies is necessary. Selecting reliable suppliers who provide high-quality ingredients and semi-prepared products ensures consistency in food quality and customer satisfaction.

Effective Advertising Strategies:
Maximize visibility through strategic advertising efforts. Eye-catching truck design serves as primary advertising, attracting random passersby. Supplemental strategies such as advertising banners in proximity to the truck's location and active social media presence further enhance brand awareness and customer engagement. Utilizing platforms like Instagram, VKontakte, and Facebook enables storytelling, promotions, giveaways, and targeted advertising to reach the desired audience.

Operational Planning:
Plan meticulously for opening and production, including obtaining all necessary permits from local authorities. Differentiate operational strategies for weekdays versus weekends, ensuring adequate stock levels to meet varying demand patterns. A comprehensive understanding of average purchase

amounts and daily foot traffic facilitates effective inventory management and operational planning.

To commence production, securing permits is imperative, as mandated by regulations governing mobile trading.

Initiate the process by drafting a letter to the local mayor's office, outlining the requisite specifications for mobile trading in your locality. This letter should include personal details and rationale for onsite vending of food items and beverages, both hot and cold.

Given the transient nature of food truck operations, it's prudent to request a comprehensive set of permits from the mayor's office to streamline the authorization process and minimize bureaucratic delays. Subsequently, maintain the entire set of obtained documents within the food truck premises and furnish them during routine inspections by local authorities.

Subsequently, select a fixed vending location for the food truck, such as a park or stadium, and obtain approval from the respective administration.

Registration as an individual entrepreneur involves liaising with the tax office or multifunctional centers. The application for individual entrepreneur registration is readily accessible online and requires declaration of specific OKVED codes pertaining to food preparation and vending activities.

During application submission, designate the preferred taxation system, preferably opting for the simplified taxation regime to mitigate potential complexities associated with general taxation, particularly with VAT considerations.

Upon individual entrepreneur registration, initiate stamp procurement, providing requisite details including full name and OGRN.

Facilitate the establishment of a current account by entering into an agreement with a bank offering favorable terms, considering provisions for free service during the initial year and nominal transaction fees.

Acquiring and registering a suitable food truck demands meticulous consideration. With diverse options available, thorough assessment is crucial. Budgetary considerations should encompass delivery expenses, particularly if situated outside the central region of Russia.

Engage a marketing agency to facilitate the selection of an attention-grabbing name, company logos, and exterior truck design. A vibrant and eye-catching food truck design is paramount, supplemented by menus, branded workwear, and advertising banners to maximize visibility and customer engagement.

Finalizing all essential agreements

The subsequent step entails finalizing lease contracts. It's crucial to comprehend that, barring participation in festivals and events, the food truck typically remains stationed at a fixed location for sales year-round.

Contact the administration to initiate lease agreements, noting that in some instances, a competitive process is involved in allocating retail spaces.

Several indispensable agreements must be formalized:

- Disinfestation and disinfection agreement
- Water supply and wastewater removal agreement
- Raw material supply contract

- Waste disposal, managed by stadium administration and incorporated into rental fees.

Securing permits from the fire inspection and Rospotrebnadzor

Furthermore, acquiring clearance from the fire inspection is imperative, with specific stipulations regarding pavilions and kiosks. Compliance mandates the presence of at least two fire extinguishers and adherence to electrical installation regulations. Additionally, food trucks necessitate automatic fire alarm systems.

Subsequently, notifying Rospotrebnadzor of the establishment's opening is mandatory. The requisite application form can be obtained from Rospotrebnadzor's official website, typically located in the "Services" section.

Staffing

Recruitment can be facilitated through popular services. Typically, two cashiers and two cooks suffice for food truck operations, with staff working in alternating shifts every two days.

Employees must undergo medical assessments to obtain sanitary certificates and comply with hygiene standards. Tailoring workwear, drafting work schedules, and providing training are also imperative.

Occupational safety training is mandatory for employees, with advance procurement of requisite journals and their organization.

To formalize employee registration, liaise with the Pension Fund of Russia and the Federal Compulsory Medical Insurance Fund.

Organizing the mobile snack bar's operations

The food truck should be outfitted with designated areas:

- Storage for staff attire, including hangers, clothing covers, and shoe containers.
- Segregated storage for detergents, ensuring separation from food storage areas.
- Water supply, comprising separate tanks for clean technical water and wastewater.

Collaborate with the chef to devise a menu and operational maps meticulously. Menu selection warrants special attention, emphasizing ease of preparation, robust flavors, and differentiation from competitors.

Creating technological maps is essential for accurately determining ingredient quantities in dishes. It's crucial to recognize that changing raw material suppliers may alter the product's taste, necessitating chefs to consistently taste-test dishes upon completion.

Choosing raw material suppliers and establishing agreements is paramount. Deliveries, occurring every two days due to limited warehouse capacity, should predominantly consist of semi-finished products. Comprehensive documentation, including invoices, veterinary certificates, and conformity certificates, must accompany deliveries, with records retained for at least a month. Exploring the market for service providers aids in selecting optimal suppliers, potentially including farmer's farms for quality meat supply.

Developing a consumer corner is imperative to avoid penalties. Essential components of this corner include the Trade Regulations Law, a complaints book, a copy of the OGRN certificate, and a log of regulatory inspections. This corner can be situated externally on the food truck or under a canopy.

Food trucks, aside from electricity, are self-sufficient, equipped with tanks for both process and waste water. Electricity connection points in public areas necessitate advance location identification and permission acquisition from administration. Generators with a minimum capacity of 9 kilowatts, along with high-capacity batteries and solar panels, ensure operational autonomy.

Attention to safety in electrical connections, spanning low-voltage (12-24 volts) and high-voltage (220 volts) equipment, is crucial. Each food truck connecting to centralized electrical networks must incorporate a grounding bus.

Waste water disposal, either through a specialized service or the stadium's technical administrative room, requires permission. Given the absence of restroom facilities in food trucks, employee restroom usage at the stadium incurs a cost.

Hot water access is facilitated via supply boilers, with water tanks exceeding 200 liters reducing water transportation needs. Water supply systems, pressurized via pumping stations equipped with pressure sensors, ensure adequate water pressure at sinks.

Modern food trucks, equipped with heating systems, are operational year-round, with kitchen operation hoods often pre-installed during equipment setup.

Acquiring technological equipment for your food truck involves engaging specialized companies to ensure quality, warranty coverage, and equipment replacement in case of malfunction. It's advisable to seek assistance from specialists for an optimal arrangement of equipment within the confined space of the food truck. This ensures employees can move comfortably without hindrance and perform their designated functions efficiently. Strategic placement of equipment near the client-serving window facilitates quick service, such as coffee machines and ice cream freezers, alongside access to refrigerated drinks.

For equipment procurement, you would need:

- Food truck: 1 unit, Price: 700,000 rubles
- Fridge: 1 unit, Price: 16,000 rubles
- Freezer: 1 unit, Price: 21,000 rubles
- Deep fryer: 1 unit, Price: 5,200 rubles
- Coffee machine: 1 unit, Price: 35,500 rubles
- Wall table: 4 units, Price: 4,300 rubles each
- Slicer: 1 unit, Price: 19,000 rubles
- Frying surface: 1 unit, Price: 17,000 rubles
- Induction cooker: 1 unit, Price: 21,000 rubles
- Grill: 1 unit, Price: 15,700 rubles
- FOC (??? Need clarification): 1 unit, Price: 19,000 rubles
- Waffle iron: 1 unit, Price: 6,000 rubles

- Ice cream freezer: 1 unit, Price: 35,000 rubles
- Electronic scales: 1 unit, Price: 1,600 rubles
- Set of kitchen utensils: 1 unit, Price: 58,000 rubles
- Cash register: 1 unit, Price: 15,700 rubles
- Sink: 1 unit, Price: 7,000 rubles
- Fire extinguisher: 2 units, Price: 3,000 rubles each
- Other expenses (e.g., cash register tapes, disposable tableware, detergents, soap dispenser, toilet paper, napkins, overalls, stamps, magazines): Total expense: 30,000 rubles
- USB modem: 1 unit, Price: 2,000 rubles

Total expense: 1,047,900 rubles.

In addition to kitchen equipment, cleaning supplies, and packaging materials for finished products are necessary. Packaging can be customized to match the enterprise's concept; for instance, special cardboard boxes and sticks enhance the appeal of WOK noodles. Special glasses with lids are essential for selling tea and coffee for takeaway.

An online cash register is essential for transactions, with various service providers offering rental options or purchase. Outsourcing accounting services eliminates the need for an in-house accountant, provided all incoming documents are meticulously collected. Internet connectivity via a USB modem from mobile operators facilitates online operations. An automated accounting system ensures accurate tracking of daily orders and income, maintaining financial control.

6. Food Truck Staff

To ensure smooth operations, a food truck requires specific personnel:

Fixed Expenses
Salary
- Cook: Monthly wage of 30,000 rubles for 2 employees, totaling 60,000 rubles.
- Cashier: Monthly wage of 25,000 rubles for 2 employees, totaling 50,000 rubles.

- Insurance Premiums: Totaling 33,000 rubles.

Total Payroll: 143,000 rubles.

At the initial stage, it's advisable not to hire a manager. However, as the business expands to multiple outlets, a manager can be recruited to oversee operations.

Cook

- Prepares dishes and assists in developing recipes.
- Undertakes preparations in the morning before peak hours.
- Supervises the cashier and provides guidance for minor food preparations.
- Ensures kitchen cleanliness.

Cashier

- Takes customer orders and communicates them to the cook.
- Manages transactions and tracks customer numbers.

- Assists the cook during low customer traffic periods.

- Prepares beverages like coffee and serves ice cream.

- Packages completed orders for customers.

Chapter 5

Attracting Customers to Your Food Truck

This section explores various strategies to draw customers to your food truck:

1. Enhance Your Food Truck's Appearance:
- Ensure your food truck has an appealing exterior design, as it significantly impacts customer attraction.
- Consider using vinyl wraps or paint to decorate your truck. Vinyl wraps are particularly effective and offer versatility in design options.

- Work with vinyl wrap companies or local artists to create eye-catching designs that reflect your brand identity and attract attention on the street.

2. Maintain Visible Hygiene:
- Prioritize cleanliness and hygiene in your food truck, as customers associate cleanliness with food quality and safety.
- Regularly clean and maintain your truck's interior and exterior to create a positive impression on customers.
- Invest in high-quality cleaning supplies and establish cleanliness protocols to uphold hygiene standards.

3. Participate in Events:
- Attend various events in your city or town to showcase your food truck and reach a larger audience.
- Events provide an excellent opportunity to introduce your food to potential customers and generate immediate interest.

- Serve your best dishes at events to leave a lasting impression and encourage repeat business from satisfied customers.

Overall, by focusing on enhancing your food truck's appearance, maintaining visible hygiene, and actively participating in events, you can effectively attract customers and grow your food truck business.

Chapter 6

Building Connections and Publicity

To expand your food truck's reach, consider the following strategies:

4. Networking:
- Registering with event organizers is essential for catering at events. However, securing spots at festivals can be competitive. To increase your chances, establish connections with event planners and follow up regularly to stay top of mind.
- Expand your network beyond event planners by reaching out to organizations that host their own events. Building relationships with key individuals

within these organizations can lead to valuable opportunities.

- Ensure your food truck operates legally, as most prospects will expect compliance with regulations before partnering with you.

5. Publicity Stunts:

- A well-executed publicity stunt can garner attention, generate buzz, and increase brand awareness. However, it's crucial to tread carefully, as stunts can backfire if poorly executed.
- Consider working with an advertising agency experienced in designing successful PR stunts to maximize impact.
- Research past publicity stunts for inspiration and adapt them to suit your brand and target market.
- Examples include hosting a cook-off or attempting to break a culinary record to engage customers and attract media attention.

6. Social Media and Online Ordering:

- Utilize social media platforms to engage with customers, share relevant content, and promote your food truck.

- Introduce online ordering options through social media, websites, or dedicated apps to streamline the purchasing process for customers.

- Developing a user-friendly menu app can provide added convenience and enhance the overall customer experience.

- Embrace digital trends to stay competitive in an increasingly digitized marketplace.

By leveraging networking opportunities, implementing creative publicity stunts, and embracing digital platforms, you can effectively attract customers and drive sales for your food truck business.

Chapter 7

Naming Your Food Truck

Selecting the right name for your food truck is a crucial step in establishing your brand identity. Here's how to choose a name that resonates with customers and sets you apart from the competition:

Why a Strong Food Truck Name Matters:
Your food truck's name is often the first point of contact with potential customers, shaping their initial impression of your business. A memorable name can attract attention and create a lasting connection with your audience, helping to build brand recognition and loyalty.

Tips for Choosing a Memorable Name:

1. Keep it Short and Memorable:

Opt for a concise and catchy name that sticks in people's minds. Consider using unique phrases or combinations of words that capture the essence of your food truck's offerings.

2. Reflect Your Cuisine:

Choose a name that reflects the type of food you serve. This not only helps customers understand what to expect but also distinguishes your truck from others in the market. Research your target audience and competitors to ensure your name stands out.

3. Know Your Audience:

Understand your target market and competitors to tailor your name accordingly. Solicit feedback from family, friends, and potential customers to gauge the appeal of different name options.

4. Consider Geographic Relevance:

Depending on your business goals, incorporating your location into the name can establish a strong local presence. However, consider future expansion plans and whether a location-specific name aligns with your long-term vision.

5. Check Domain Name Availability:

Before finalizing a name, verify that the associated domain name and social media handles are available. Avoid potential conflicts or confusion by ensuring consistency across online platforms.

Ultimately, the right name for your food truck should encapsulate your brand identity, resonate with your target audience, and leave a lasting impression on customers. With these considerations in mind, you can confidently choose a name that sets your food truck apart in the competitive culinary landscape.

25 Food Truck Name Suggestions:

1. Roaming Kitchen
2. Blaze Road Grill
3. Ravenous Woodsman
4. Wrap Haven
5. Fry Force
6. Flavor Expedition
7. Rolling Gourmets
8. Cheeky Swine
9. Pete's Rest Stop
10. Divine Crêpe!
11. Doughnut Delight
12. Tasty Tacos Express
13. Bao Bliss
14. Artisan Grilled Cheese Co.
15. Meatball Syndicate
16. Sushi Roll Mobile
17. Veggie Oasis
18. Street Bite Sliders
19. Let's Feast!
20. Flaky Cruiser

21. Toasted Roastwagon
22. Quesadilla Quarters
23. Biscuit Brigade
24. Smoothie Station
25. Dumpling Dive

What to Do After Choosing Your Food Truck Name:

1. Research and Select the Ideal Location: Choose a spot with high foot traffic and visibility to attract more customers.
2. Secure Financing: Whether through loans, investors, or personal savings, ensure you have adequate funds to cover startup costs.
3. Obtain Necessary Licenses and Permits: Ensure compliance with local regulations by obtaining all required permits and licenses.
4. Acquire or Rent a Food Truck: Equip it with essential equipment and supplies.

5. Promote Your Business: Establish an online presence through social media and digital marketing channels.

6. Develop Your Menu: Craft a menu featuring high-quality ingredients sourced from local suppliers.

FAQ:

How to Pick a Food Truck Company Name?

Select a name that reflects your food theme and style, opting for clever puns or memorable phrases. Keep it concise and easy to remember.

What Are Popular Food Truck Food Items?

Tacos, sandwiches, burgers, gourmet hot dogs, and fusion cuisine are popular choices. Offer something unique to differentiate yourself.

How Can I Attract Customers to My Food Truck?

Utilize social media, build relationships with local businesses, leverage existing networks, and provide exceptional customer service.

Chapter 8

Crafting Your Food Truck Menu

Embarking on your food truck journey brings forth a realm of possibilities: mobility, innovation, and the thrill of exploring new locations. Yet, before you hit the road, there's a crucial element you need: a well-crafted menu.

Your menu, whether displayed physically or digitally, serves as a vital tool for engaging customers and maximizing profits. Beyond just listing items, it's an opportunity to showcase your brand identity through design, colors, and layout. If you're feeling daunted by the task, fear not. This guide will walk you through the essential menu design practices tailored for your unique food truck venture.

Best Practices for Food Truck Menu Design

In this section, we'll delve into key menu design practices to help you create a visually appealing and effective menu for your food truck.

Creating Your Food Truck Menu

Here are ten steps to guide you through the process of designing a captivating menu for your food truck:

1. Compile Your Menu Items
Start by listing all the items you plan to offer on your menu. Given the niche focus and limited space of food trucks, your menu may be more concise compared to traditional restaurants. However, this doesn't limit your creativity. Consider every aspect of your offerings, from proteins and toppings for tacos to milk substitutions and flavor syrups for coffee. Don't forget to include any special deals or exclusive items to add intrigue for your customers.

Take your time with this step to ensure you capture every potential purchase option.

2. Organize Menu Items Into Categories

The next consideration is how to categorize your menu items. Even with a compact menu suitable for a food truck, this step remains crucial, laying the groundwork for your overall menu design. Will you opt for a customizable approach, allowing customers to build their own tacos with various proteins and toppings, or will you offer a set taco menu without modifications? Additionally, if combo plates are on offer, will you detail each component or focus solely on the available combinations? Strategically organizing your items can enhance your menu's appeal and help highlight top-selling or premium items, ultimately optimizing revenue generation.

3. Establish Menu Pricing

Setting menu prices should be a deliberate process, taking various factors into account. Considerations include alignment with your target market's preferences and affordability, ensuring prices are conducive to repeat business. It's essential to strike a balance between affordability and profitability, ensuring that revenue covers all operational expenses. This entails thorough consideration of staffing, maintenance, inventory, and other overhead costs. Conducting a competitive analysis of food truck pricing in your area is vital to positioning your prices appropriately based on quality, innovation, and unique value propositions.

4. Craft Menu Descriptions

Once items are listed, categorized, and priced, attention turns to crafting compelling menu descriptions. Reflect on the most effective communication methods: concise or detailed descriptions, or perhaps reliance on vibrant imagery. Consider the tone you wish to convey—whether straightforward or infused with humor. Additionally, account for dietary considerations by including allergy information or nutrition details either directly on the menu or available upon request. Put yourself in the customer's shoes to anticipate their informational needs, and if needed, enlist the expertise of a copywriter to enhance your menu descriptions.

5. Select a Menu Color Palette

Transitioning to the creative aspect of menu design, consider choosing a suitable color scheme. Evaluate existing branding elements you might possess, such as logos, fonts, and colors, which can inform your menu's visual identity. Alternatively, if you're still refining your brand, contemplate which colors would best represent your business and align with your desired aesthetic. Determine the number of colors to include, considering whether bright, attention-grabbing hues are appropriate or if a more subdued palette would be preferable to avoid overwhelming visuals. Resources like Chron's "The Psychology of Colors for Restaurant Designs" and tools like Adobe Color CC and ColorDot can provide inspiration for crafting your color scheme. Additionally, bear in mind that black and white printing is often more cost-effective than color, so factor in printing costs if planning to produce numerous menu copies.

6. Craft Your Food Truck Menu Design

Utilize platforms like Canva and Adobe Suite, along with available templates, to initiate your menu design. Social media platforms such as Pinterest, Instagram, and TikTok can also serve as valuable sources of inspiration for menu design concepts. Consider practical aspects like available space on your truck and how to effectively convey essential information without overcrowding the menu. Ensure readability and ease of navigation, with clearly labeled sections and prominently displayed prices. Differentiate between printed or digital menu versions and the menu displayed on your food truck, determining what additional details to include in supplementary formats.

7. Incorporate Food Truck Menu Photography

Enhance customer engagement and drive sales by showcasing high-quality photos of your menu items. Visual previews of your offerings can significantly influence customer behavior and generate excitement about your food truck. For some food trucks, particularly those with visually appealing dishes, relying primarily on photos as the main menu format can be an effective strategy. However, prioritize using professionally shot, high-quality images to maintain the integrity and credibility of your brand. If incorporating photos into the food truck menu isn't feasible, consider including them in printed or digital menu versions or linking to a digital menu via a QR code. Leverage the power of social media to amplify your menu's reach and generate buzz around your food truck, utilizing platforms like TikTok to attract new customers and capitalize on social currency to drive sales.

8. Decide on Menu Typography, Spacing, and Layout

Consider the final visual elements for your menu: typography, spacing, and overall layout. Reflect on how these choices will align with the overall aesthetic of your food truck. Will you opt for playful or more formal fonts, or perhaps a blend of both styles? Determine whether you'll use a single font throughout your menu or incorporate multiple styles and sizes. If choosing different fonts, decide on their placement and how they contribute to the overall visual appeal.

In terms of spacing, strategize how to structure your menu to ensure clarity and readability while avoiding overcrowding. Will you maintain uniform spacing or deliberately adjust it to evoke a specific atmosphere? Consider where to integrate images within the layout—will you include actual photographs or employ creative illustrations of your menu items? Keep in mind that your menu is a dynamic aspect of your business that may evolve over time, so allow flexibility for future adjustments and enjoy the creative process.

9. Finalize the Menu Design

After experimenting with various design elements, colors, fonts, and layouts, it's time to select the definitive menu design. Seek input from your network, including stakeholders, staff, friends, and family, to gather feedback on the different options. Incorporate any valuable suggestions into your design before proceeding to finalize it for printing or display on your food truck.

10. Proofread and Print the Menu

Before proceeding further, meticulously proofread your menu to catch any errors, such as spelling mistakes or typos. Enlist the help of others to ensure a thorough review and eliminate any oversight. Once you've confirmed the accuracy of the content, proceed with printing if opting for a physical menu. Explore printing services offered by companies like Staples, Vistaprint, PsPrint, or PrintPlace to find the most suitable option for your menu printing needs. With the menu design finalized and printed, congratulations are in order—enjoy your culinary journey!

Chapter 9

Establishing Your Food Truck Brand

Setting your food truck apart from the competition is essential for attracting and retaining a loyal customer base. Branding goes beyond mere logos and names—it's about creating a memorable identity and narrative that resonates with your audience.

Understanding Branding

Branding, or brand marketing, focuses on cultivating and showcasing a company's unique brand identity, core values, and commitments to stand out in the market. It involves employing strategies to foster a positive image of the company's offerings, aiming to cultivate loyalty, trust, and preference among consumers.

Let's take a closer look at a prime example of effective branding: Pizza Hut. Pizza Hut's relaxed brand image resonates well with its target audience, particularly the youth. Consistency is evident across various touchpoints, from the restaurant ambiance to delivery trucks and packaging, highlighting the importance of maintaining brand colors and identity.

Developing Your Food Truck Brand Identity
Crafting a distinct brand identity is crucial for every new food truck venture. The goal is to attract potential customers and cultivate their loyalty through consistency in branding.

Brand consistency is vital. It ensures that your brand stands out and remains appealing to your target audience. However, branding is not just about appearances; it's also about delivering on the brand promise. Building brand loyalty requires offering high-quality products and services that align with your brand identity.

Maintaining Consistency Across Channels

What makes a food truck brand memorable? Similar to established brands like Coke or McDonald's, consistency is key. This includes maintaining consistent colors, a distinct brand voice, memorable logos, and unique slogans across all mediums. Food trucks follow a similar pattern, emphasizing the importance of these elements along with other strategic considerations to build a strong brand presence.

Steps to Develop Your Food Truck's Brand Identity:

1. Work with a graphic designer to create a comprehensive brand guide that encompasses your food truck's logo, colors, and all design elements. Consistency across platforms is key.

2. Select colors that reflect your brand's essence and apply them consistently across all design elements for a cohesive appearance. A well-defined visual brand is crucial for success.

3. Ensure fonts, images, and packaging align with your brand's aesthetic to enhance recognition.

4. Integrate your brand identity into your food truck's design and any physical spaces you occupy to maintain a cohesive theme.

5. Standardize all materials, including business cards and online profiles, to reinforce your brand identity.

6. Train your team on your brand guidelines to ensure uniformity in logo usage, color schemes, and other design elements.

7. Regularly review your branding to ensure consistency and alignment with your food truck's values and offerings.

8. Establish a unified visual theme for all marketing materials and digital platforms.

9. Develop a distinct brand voice for all communications to effectively engage your target audience.

10. Utilize social media marketing to showcase your food truck's offerings and provide behind-the-scenes insights.

11. Consider offering branded merchandise or packaging to extend your food truck's visibility beyond its physical location.

Consistent branding simplifies recognition and recall for customers, ensuring that every interaction with your brand conveys your values and aesthetics, creating a cohesive and memorable brand experience.

Every food truck brand will carve out its unique niche, and your branding should encapsulate something special to set your food truck apart as a distinctive culinary destination.

Offline and Online Branding:

Examine how Pizza Hut maintains consistency across both online and offline platforms, with buttons and images reflecting their brand colors. Consistency is vital for brand integrity.

Here are some top strategies for branding both online and offline, helping you stand out from the competition:

Online Branding for Food Trucks:

Utilizing digital platforms is a cost-effective way to promote your mobile food brand. Sharing appetizing food images online is free, and starting an online ad campaign is typically easier and less expensive than offline alternatives.

Best Practices for Online Branding for Food Trucks:

1. Establish a Website: Utilize a restaurant website builder to create a website that highlights your food truck's brand. Ensure it includes high-quality images, a clear mission statement, easy navigation, and a mobile-responsive layout.

2. Utilize Social Media Marketing: Identify the social media platforms where your target audience

is most active and establish a strong presence there to engage with potential customers.

3. Create a Mobile App: Utilize a restaurant app builder to develop a mobile app for your food truck. This app can be used to send push notifications about your location, special offers, and other updates directly to your customers.

4. Foster Customer Loyalty: Implement a restaurant loyalty program to incentivize repeat visits. Offer rewards such as a free meal or discounts after a certain number of purchases.

5. Focus on SEO: Start a blog to share recipes, stories, or cooking tips related to your food truck's offerings. This not only enhances your restaurant's SEO but also positions your brand as an authority in the food industry.

6. Implement Email Marketing: Collect email addresses from your customers and send out

newsletters to keep them informed about your food truck's latest offerings and updates.

7. Manage Online Reviews: Encourage customers to leave online reviews and respond to their feedback professionally. Implementing a restaurant feedback system can help streamline this process.

8. Utilize Online Advertising: Invest in online ads to target potential customers in your local area and increase awareness of your food truck.

9. Collaborate with Influencers: Partner with local influencers who resonate with your target audience to expand your reach and attract new customers.

10. Analyze Performance: Keep track of your online presence and customer engagement using restaurant analytics tools to identify areas for improvement and optimize your marketing strategies.

Offline Branding Strategies for Food Trucks:

Offline promotion continues to play a fundamental role in food truck marketing, facilitating connections with local communities and attracting customers who may not yet be engaged with your brand online. These strategies focus on tangible interactions and experiences to enhance brand visibility and recognition.

Best Practices for Offline Food Truck Branding:

1. Customized Packaging: Reflect your brand's identity through tailored packaging that aligns with your theme, whether it's vibrant and lively for street foods or sleek and minimalist for gourmet offerings.

2. Seasonal Flyers: Utilize flyers to promote special deals or seasonal menu items, ensuring the design and messaging resonate with your brand image.

3. Personalized Delivery: Make your delivery service memorable by incorporating personal touches like handwritten notes or complimentary samples, ensuring that each order arrives in optimal condition.

4. Sampling Events: Host tasting events where potential customers can sample your signature dishes, providing them with a direct experience of what distinguishes your food truck.

5. Collaborations: Partner with local businesses for joint promotional efforts, creating exclusive combos or discounts that benefit both your customer bases.

6. Interactive Packaging: Utilize QR codes on your packaging to provide access to exclusive online content such as recipes, your food truck's story, or upcoming location schedules.

7. Pop-up Appearances: Take advantage of your food truck's mobility by appearing at events, festivals, or hosting collaborative pop-ups with other businesses. Always have promotional materials readily available to encourage repeat visits.

8. Branded Signage: Invest in branded signage to attract customers and reinforce brand recognition, ensuring consistency across all visual elements.

9. Food Truck Design: Customize your food truck to reflect your branding effectively. Your truck should clearly communicate your mission statement and brand identity through its design and appearance.

Top Food Truck Branding Examples:

Here are some inspiring examples of successful food truck branding:

1. Kogi BBQ: Kogi BBQ maintains consistent branding across its website, social media platforms, and physical food truck, showcasing its recognizable logo and brand identity.

2. The Lobos Truck: The Lobos Truck utilizes consistent colors and branding elements across all platforms to enhance brand recognition and visibility.

3. The Tropic Truck: The Tropic Truck stands out with bold truck design and cohesive branding both online and offline, ensuring that its presence is unmistakable across all channels.

Key Takeaways:
- Food truck branding is essential for building customer loyalty and should focus on creating a memorable identity and narrative that resonates with the audience emotionally.
- Developing a cohesive brand identity involves elements such as a distinctive logo, thematic

visuals, consistent brand tone, and branded merchandise or packaging.

- Maintaining consistency in branding across various platforms, both online and offline, is crucial for reinforcing brand recognition and fostering customer loyalty.

- Offline branding strategies encompass personalized packaging, seasonal promotions, customized delivery experiences, tasting events, collaborations, interactive displays, and pop-up locations.

Chapter 10

Determining the Ideal Number of Menu Items for Your Food Truck

Embarking on the journey of launching a food truck involves crafting a distinctive menu that encapsulates your culinary vision. This menu serves as the heart of your mobile restaurant, shaping its identity and flavor profile.

Although the temptation to offer an extensive menu is strong, most food truck operators typically feature a selection of 6 to 12 items. But how many dishes should you include on your food truck menu? Here's a guide to help you create a menu that is both enticing and economically viable.

Identify Key Menu Items

The initial step in menu creation is selecting a handful of core items. These dishes should serve as the foundation of your food truck's offerings, enticing customers to return for more. Conduct market research to ensure that your menu stands out from competitors.

Focus on a cohesive theme for your central dishes. Whether it's sandwiches or French cuisine, maintain a unified concept. For example, your menu could feature raclette grilled cheese, croque madame, jambon-beurre, and pan bagnat to blend both concepts seamlessly.

Consider Preparation Time

While flavorful dishes are essential, practicality is paramount for a successful food truck menu. Your signature raclette grilled cheese might yield a high profit margin, but if it takes 20 minutes to prepare, efficiency becomes a concern. Conversely, simpler options like jambon-beurre, comprising basic ingredients, offer quicker turnaround times.

It's crucial to strike a balance between complexity and efficiency. Even if a gourmet dish is profitable, it must be feasible within your kitchen's capabilities. Unless you aim to compete with upscale eateries, prioritize simplicity to streamline operations, especially during peak hours.

Stay Grounded

Maintaining a realistic outlook is essential for your food truck's prosperity. If your operating hours are limited to lunchtime, offering an extensive menu is impractical. Simplifying your offerings ensures smoother service and minimizes waste.

Opt for a streamlined menu to expedite service. For instance, if your specialty is hotdogs and brats, limit side options to essentials like French fries and grilled corn. This approach maximizes efficiency and reduces operational complexity.

Tailor Your Approach

There's no universal formula for determining the ideal number of menu items. While many food trucks feature 6 to 12 dishes, prioritize quality over quantity. Factor in preparation times and logistical considerations to curate a menu that aligns with your business model.

By customizing your menu to suit your food truck's capabilities and customer preferences, you can optimize efficiency and enhance the overall dining experience.

Chapter 11

Top-Selling Food Truck Items

Operating a food truck is an exciting venture in today's thriving American mobile dining scene. However, success in this industry requires strategic menu choices to ensure profitability. To help propel your food truck business forward, we've compiled a list of the top 10 most lucrative food truck items for the current year. By incorporating these dishes into your menu, you can drive revenue and achieve success wherever your culinary journey takes you.

Before diving into the list, it's essential to recognize the significance of technology in modern food truck operations. A robust POS (Point of Sale) system serves as the backbone of your business, facilitating efficient order management, menu updates across multiple trucks, and reliable service around the clock. Cutting-edge hardware solutions like Otter POS are specifically tailored to streamline operations in compact kitchen spaces, enabling you to maximize productivity and profitability. With the right technological tools in place, your food truck is primed for success.

10. Fish & Chips

Hailing from the shores of the British Isles, fish & chips have emerged as a beloved street food staple in the United States. From bustling street food festivals in cities like Austin to iconic coastal destinations such as Venice Beach, fish & chip trucks have garnered widespread popularity. Even esteemed culinary professionals, like Queen Elizabeth's former personal chef, are embracing this trend by offering crispy, flavorful seafood sourced directly from the West Coast. If your food truck is equipped with a frying station, you have the perfect opportunity to delight customers with delicious fish

& chips as they embark on their culinary adventures.

9. Breakfasts

Food trucks have proven to be lucrative ventures at any time of day, and the rising popularity of mobile breakfast offerings underscores this fact. In 2023, prominent restaurant chains like Taco Bell began heavily investing in breakfast-focused food trucks, positioning themselves to compete with fast-casual coffee chains. The breakfast truck trend allows businesses to explore innovative concepts, particularly in high-revenue states such as California and Texas, making them a favorable option for operators. Since most breakfast items can be prepared and served within minutes, these trucks achieve profitability well before noon.

8. Fried Chicken

Fried chicken has emerged as one of the fastest-growing segments in the American fast-food industry since the mid-2010s. Consequently, numerous fried chicken establishments are taking their operations to the streets. Established brands like Wings N' Things have become fixtures at local food truck festivals, alongside a plethora of new startups. Similar to fish & chips, fried chicken is easily and quickly prepared in any food truck setup. This enables operators to efficiently cater to large crowds at festivals and outdoor events, maximizing profitability.

7. Ice Cream

Few food truck concepts garner as much adoration as those offering ice cream. The recent resurgence of retro ice cream trucks has propelled this segment of the industry into a new era of popularity. Ice cream trucks have long been beloved by customers, thanks to their nostalgic appeal and convenient, prepackaged treats. With desserts that require minimal preparation and cooking, these trucks can easily portion and sell their offerings without extensive culinary equipment. With the ice cream industry poised to exceed $2.6 billion in revenue by 2030, there's never been a more opportune moment to enter the market and start scooping up profits.

6. Mexican Food

In 2024, approximately 1 in 10 food trucks feature Mexican cuisine on their menus, highlighting its widespread popularity. Tacos, burritos, and Mexican bowls have been mainstays of food truck fare for decades and have experienced a surge in demand in recent years. These dishes often share ingredients, allowing for fast and flexible preparation without incurring high overhead costs. Additionally, the preference for spicy flavors among Millennials and Gen Z further contributes to the success of Mexican food trucks, making them valuable assets for operators seeking to cater to diverse tastes.

5. Grilled Cheese Sandwiches

Grilled cheese sandwiches offer one of the highest profit-to-cost ratios in the food truck industry. With basic ingredients readily available at low costs, these sandwiches can be prepared fresh in mere minutes, making them ideal for quick service from compact kitchen spaces. What sets grilled cheese sandwiches apart is their customizability. Utilizing digital menu management tools, operators can experiment with various ingredients or allow customers to create their own personalized sandwiches. As grilled cheese trucks continue to innovate, they are poised to emerge as leaders in the industry's profitability landscape.

4. Cupcakes

Forbes has forecasted cupcake retailers to become the most profitable business type in 2024, and cupcake trucks are already establishing themselves as highly successful dessert enterprises across the United States. Food truck operators are infusing their unique twists into this beloved sweet treat, contributing to each business's distinct identity. Much like other profitable food truck items, cupcakes are easy to prepare ahead of service, quick to serve, and offer ample opportunities for customization, ensuring continued popularity among customers.

3. Indian Food

Indian cuisine, particularly dishes from the Punjabi culture, has been gaining prominence in the American culinary scene. Now, food truck adaptations of favorites like tandoori chicken and papri chaat are emerging as success stories within the mobile dining industry. In 2023, Indian food trucks ranked among the most profitable in the country, with growing demand anticipated. Cities renowned for their food truck culture, such as Portland and Austin, are witnessing an increasing presence of Indian street food, introducing these vibrant flavors to new and eager audiences.

2. Barbecue (BBQ)

While BBQ may have slipped from its top ranking in 2023, it remains a highly profitable option for food truck owners. Many of the most successful food truck businesses continue to feature BBQ on their menus, maintaining its widespread popularity among diners nationwide. This trend is particularly pronounced in states renowned for their love of BBQ, such as South Carolina and Texas, where BBQ trucks consistently outperform their competitors.

1. Burgers

Claiming the title of the most profitable food truck item for 2024 is the beloved classic: burgers! Burgers have long been a staple of food truck fare, and they continue to reign as the top-selling item in the mobile dining industry. Regardless of the type of food truck you operate, there's always space for a burger with your own unique twist. A well-crafted burger recipe not only attracts the most orders but also generates the highest profit margins among all cuisines. By featuring burgers on your menu, your food truck can effectively compete in the dynamic and expanding food truck market, positioning itself for success.

Boost Your Food Truck's Profitability

Now armed with insights into the cravings of today's on-the-go diners and the items they're willing to pay for, you can maximize the profitability of your food truck. While competition may be fierce, a strategic approach will help your mobile dining business thrive in any environment. Select the right items from the aforementioned list that complement your truck's concept and culinary offerings, and infuse them with your own unique flair. Leveraging excellent cooking skills, robust technology, and active customer engagement, you can optimize your food truck's profitability and secure its success in the ever-evolving food truck landscape.

Chapter 12

Selecting Profitable Food for Your Food Truck

Key Considerations for Choosing the Most Lucrative Food Options for a Food Truck:

1. Understanding Your Customer Base

Gaining insight into your target market is pivotal in determining the most appealing food choices. Delve into their preferences, demographics, and cultural inclinations through methods such as market research, customer engagement, and participation in local events. This exploration will provide valuable data on their culinary desires and tastes.

2. Cost-Efficient Ingredients

The cost of ingredients significantly impacts your bottom line. Scrutinize ingredient prices and their accessibility. Opt for food items that utilize cost-effective ingredients without compromising on flavor or quality. This strategy ensures competitive pricing without sacrificing profit margins.

3. Efficiency in Preparation

Operational efficiency is paramount for a food truck enterprise. Choose food options that are easy to prepare, especially during peak periods when demand is high. Elaborate dishes requiring extensive preparation or cooking times may not align with the limited space and time constraints of a food truck setting.

4. Gauging Food Popularity

Assess the popularity of various food choices within your locale. Analyze prevailing food trends, conduct market surveys, and review competitors' menus. By identifying and capitalizing on high-demand food items, you can broaden your customer base and enhance profitability.

5. Evaluating Competition

Survey the landscape of food truck and restaurant competition in your vicinity. Take note of their offered cuisines and pinpoint gaps or niches where your food truck can excel. While offering popular fare is crucial, integrating a unique twist or specialty item can distinguish your offerings from competitors.

6. Seasonal Adaptation

Consider the influence of seasonal shifts on consumer food preferences. Tailor your menu to incorporate seasonal specialties, aligning with fluctuating demand. For instance, summer may favor refreshing options like salads or frozen treats, while winter might embrace heartier comfort foods.

7. Personal Expertise and Passion

Harness your culinary skills and personal interests in the selection of profitable food offerings for your food truck. Opt for dishes that resonate with your culinary passions and expertise, as this enthusiasm translates into the quality of your offerings. Your mastery of specific cuisines or cooking techniques can serve as a unique selling proposition for your food truck.

Profitable Food Choices for Your Food Truck

1. BBQ Delights

Barbecue cuisine stands as a perennial crowd-pleaser, renowned for its smoky and robust flavors. Offering classics like ribs, pulled pork, or brisket, barbecue dishes attract a wide audience. With its slow-cooking method and batch-preparation suitability, barbecue is conducive to the operational dynamics of a food truck. Moreover, the affordability of ingredients, encompassing meat cuts, spices, and sauces, ensures favorable profit margins.

2. Taco Varieties

Tacos boast remarkable versatility, accommodating a plethora of creative fillings and flavor profiles. Their universal appeal spans across diverse demographics, catering to meat enthusiasts, vegetarians, and vegans alike. Quick assembly and ingredient accessibility make tacos well-suited for the fast-paced environment of a food truck. Additionally, the cost-effectiveness of staple ingredients such as tortillas, meats, and toppings facilitates a lucrative cost structure.

3. Gourmet Grilled Cheese

Grilled cheese sandwiches epitomize comfort food indulgence, eliciting nostalgia and satisfaction. With a canvas of various breads, cheeses, and fillings, the possibilities for culinary experimentation are endless. The simplicity of preparation and minimal equipment requirements make grilled cheese sandwiches an ideal choice for food truck operations. Moreover, the affordability of ingredients underscores their profitability potential.

4. Falafel Fusion

Falafel, a staple of Middle Eastern street cuisine, presents a health-conscious and flavorful option for discerning customers, particularly those seeking vegetarian or vegan fare. Crafted from ground chickpeas, herbs, and spices, falafel balls offer versatility in presentation, whether tucked in pita bread or served with an array of accompaniments. The ease of preparation, aided by pre-made mixes, and the cost-effectiveness of ingredients contribute to its appeal among food truck patrons.

5. Classic Mac and Cheese

Mac and cheese, a timeless comfort classic, exerts a universal allure transcending age demographics. Its velvety cheese goodness lends itself to endless variations, enhanced by imaginative toppings such as bacon or breadcrumbs. The straightforward preparation process and favorable cost-to-profit ratio position mac and cheese as a favored choice among food truck offerings.

6. Frozen Treats

During the warmer months, frozen delights like ice cream remain a perennial favorite among customers seeking a cooling indulgence. A diverse array of ice cream flavors, sundaes, and innovative offerings such as ice cream sandwiches can entice a broad clientele. Managing the costs of ice cream ingredients effectively ensures appealing profit margins. To differentiate your offerings, explore unique flavor blends and premium toppings.

7. Artisanal Beverages

Harnessing the popularity of coffee and tea, particularly among discerning consumers, can yield substantial profits for your food truck venture. Investing in premium coffee beans or tea leaves enables the provision of specialty drinks such as espresso-based beverages, lattes, and herbal infusions. With suitable equipment and training, you can serve up a satisfying caffeine fix on the go, with ample room for markup contributing to overall profitability.

8. Refreshing Smoothies

Catering to health-conscious patrons, smoothies have emerged as sought-after options, especially in warmer climates. Crafting a menu featuring a diverse range of fruit and vegetable-based smoothies empowers customers to customize their blends. Incorporating nutritious elements like superfoods, protein enhancements, or dairy-free alternatives caters to varied dietary preferences. Utilizing fresh ingredients and crafting enticing flavor combinations can transform smoothies into a profitable offering, particularly during peak seasons.

9. Tempting Pastries

Donuts, a beloved breakfast or snack staple, present a reliable avenue for generating profits from your food truck. Their widespread appeal and indulgent allure ensure a steady stream of customers throughout the day. Offering an assortment of flavors, glazes, fillings, and toppings accommodates diverse taste preferences. With basic ingredients like flour, sugar, yeast, and oil, donuts boast cost-effective production, facilitating healthy profit margins, especially when paired with upscale or gourmet variants commanding premium prices.

10. Upscale Burger Creations

Injecting sophistication into the traditional burger paradigm through premium ingredients, inventive flavor profiles, and imaginative toppings can elevate your food truck's appeal. Experimenting with gourmet meat blends like wagyu or grass-fed beef and diversifying with vegetarian or vegan alternatives broadens your market reach. Incorporating tantalizing toppings such as artisanal cheeses, caramelized onions, avocado, or signature sauces enhances the gourmet burger experience. Capitalizing on the potential for higher pricing, gourmet burgers can substantially enhance profitability.

Remember, while these suggestions provide a solid foundation for your food truck menu, customization based on your market, location, and customer preferences is essential for sustained success.

Chapter 13

Assessing Food Truck Profitability

Investment Requirements

Establishing a mobile snack bar necessitates the allocation of financial resources for various components:

1. Registration and Permits: 50,000 rubles.
2. Food Truck Design Project: 38,000 rubles.
3. Repair Costs: 10,000 rubles.
4. Branding Expenses (truck stickers, menu): 30,000 rubles.
5. Cash Register Equipment Registration: 3,600 rubles.
6. Advertising (banner printing, installation, rental space, social media): 28,000 rubles.

7. Automated Accounting System: 13,000 rubles.
8. Fire Alarm Installation: 8,800 rubles.
9. Food Truck Security Alarm: 13,000 rubles.
10. Rent: 150,000 rubles.
11. Technological Equipment Layout: 15,000 rubles.
12. Equipment Procurement: 1,047,900 rubles.
13. Miscellaneous Expenses: 3,000 rubles.

Total Investment: 1,410,300 rubles.

Monthly Expenditures

Ongoing monthly expenses encompass various operational aspects:

1. Payroll (including deductions): 143,000 rubles.
2. Rent: 75,000 rubles.
3. Depreciation: 1,611 rubles.
4. Process Water Procurement: 3,600 rubles.
5. Electricity: 18,000 rubles.
6. Advertising: 20,000 rubles.
7. Internet: 1,500 rubles.

8. Remote Accounting Services: 5,000 rubles.

9. Goods Purchase: 728,507 rubles.

10. Household Expenses: 5,000 rubles.

11. Contingency Fund: 3,000 rubles.

Total Monthly Expenses: 1,004,218 rubles.

Monthly Expenses Structure

This business model remains profitable even during off-peak seasons, boasting a 37% profitability rate and a 17% discount rate. The project achieves breakeven within 7 months.

Chapter 14

Identifying Risk Factors

Equipment Malfunction

Failure of technological equipment poses a significant risk, potentially leading to loss of sales. When entering into agreements with equipment suppliers, ensure to scrutinize clauses concerning the provision of replacement equipment in case of breakdowns. This precautionary measure safeguards against disruptions to your operations during equipment repairs.

Client Decline due to Weather Conditions

Food truck clientele primarily comprises pedestrians, rendering them susceptible to fluctuations in weather conditions. Inclement weather often correlates with a sharp decline in sales. To mitigate this risk, always have contingency plans in place. For instance, securing a backup location near a large shopping center ensures access to an alternative customer base, particularly during adverse weather conditions when foot traffic increases indoors.

Substandard Raw Materials

Inadequate quality of raw materials compromises the taste and appeal of your products, rendering advertising efforts and distinctive branding ineffective. Mitigate this risk by meticulously selecting suppliers and conducting rigorous quality inspections of finished products. Prioritizing quality ensures consistency in product excellence and customer satisfaction.

Legislative Changes Impacting Food Trucks

As regulations governing food truck operations evolve, compliance becomes paramount to avoid fines and penalties. Stay vigilant about legislative changes and amendments affecting food truck operations. Proactively adapting to new requirements ensures continued legal adherence and mitigates the risk of regulatory non-compliance.

Chapter 15

Understanding the Primary Objective of a Food Truck

The overarching goals of a food truck business mirror those of a traditional restaurant, albeit with distinctive nuances specific to the mobile culinary landscape. Delving into this dynamic sector, here are seven pivotal objectives for aspiring food truck entrepreneurs:

1. Cultivating a Robust Customer Base
Diversity thrives within the food truck realm, showcasing an array of cuisines and innovative culinary presentations. Success often stems from offering a unique dining experience. Therefore, it's

essential to conduct thorough market research to identify unmet customer demands and avoid overlapping offerings. Considerations include:

- Defining your culinary niche.
- Assessing existing competitors within your chosen cuisine.
- Crafting a distinctive selling proposition for your offerings.
- Strategizing optimal locations to maximize foot traffic.

For instance, envisioning a hot dog-centric food truck warrants scrutiny of existing hot dog vendors and brainstorming novel approaches to stand out in the market. Securing a strategic location bustling with pedestrian activity remains imperative, as visibility plays a pivotal role in attracting clientele.

2. Enhancing Sales and Profitability

Following the establishment of a strong customer base, the next objective revolves around amplifying sales and profitability. Diversifying your service locations beyond regular street vending opportunities can unlock new revenue streams. Explore avenues such as catering for private events, weddings, and birthday celebrations to expand your clientele.

Leveraging social media platforms can augment your promotional efforts, heightening brand visibility and stimulating sales. Initiating positive publicity campaigns facilitates customer engagement and fosters brand loyalty. Additionally, strategic pricing adjustments, offering premium menu items, and introducing supplementary services like catering or delivery can bolster revenue generation.

Amidst these endeavors, prioritizing customer satisfaction remains paramount. Ensuring a delightful dining experience fosters repeat business and cultivates a loyal customer base, underpinning long-term success in achieving sales and profit targets.

3. Minimize Food Waste

Efforts to reduce food waste not only benefit the environment but also contribute to the financial health of your food truck venture. Managing waste efficiently can lead to cost savings and increased profitability, given the perishable nature of food inventory in this industry. Collaborating with fellow food truck operators can provide valuable insights into waste reduction strategies.

Careful menu planning is instrumental in minimizing waste by accurately gauging ingredient requirements for each event or shift. Maximizing ingredient utilization, such as repurposing surplus ingredients creatively, aids in waste reduction. Additional waste reduction tactics include offering smaller portion sizes, utilizing inventory tracking software, practicing proper food storage techniques to prevent spoilage, and exploring opportunities for food donation to community organizations.

4. Secure Prime Locations

Strategic placement plays a pivotal role in the success of your food truck enterprise. Identifying and accessing high-traffic venues such as festivals, concerts, and sporting events can significantly boost sales. Cultivating partnerships with local businesses for on-site vending opportunities expands your customer reach. Engaging with food truck associations and online platforms like StreetFoodFinder.com facilitates location discovery and enhances visibility.

5. Uphold Food Safety Standards

Maintaining adherence to food safety regulations is paramount for business continuity and reputation preservation. Acquiring and upholding safety certifications ensures compliance with city and county health department guidelines. Collaborating with local food truck associations fosters knowledge sharing and regulatory compliance awareness among industry peers.

6. Explore Brick-and-Mortar Expansion

Transitioning from a food truck to a brick-and-mortar establishment is a strategic decision that warrants meticulous market analysis and financial assessment. Factors to consider include operational longevity, profitability metrics, competitor landscape, resilience to economic fluctuations, and readiness for increased overhead costs.

7. Foster Supplier Relationships

Cultivating strong relationships with suppliers is instrumental in securing quality ingredients at competitive prices. Identifying reliable vendors and leveraging their offerings optimally contributes to the operational efficiency and success of your food truck business.

Conclusion

Operating a food truck presents both challenges and opportunities in equal measure. Key strategies such as strategic location selection, networking within the industry, and participation in special events contribute to business growth and sustainability. With careful planning and continuous adaptation, your food truck venture can evolve into a thriving enterprise, offering a menu of success to both you and your customers.

www.ingramcontent.com/pod-product-compliance
Lightning Source LLC
Chambersburg PA
CBHW070258230526
45470CB00002B/639